for Monas[...]

Miss B. Mayne

Frontispiece. Montecassino as rebuilt by Abbot Desiderius, 1066–77. (Restoration drawing by K. J. C.)

Benedictine Contributions
To Church Architecture

By Kenneth John Conant

Wimmer Lecture, 1947

THE ARCHABBEY PRESS
Latrobe, Pennsylvania
1949

OBLATES OF ST BENEDICT

COPYRIGHT, 1949, BY SAINT VINCENT ARCHABBEY
PRINTED IN THE UNITED STATES OF AMERICA

Wimmer Lecture I

Saint Vincent College, Latrobe, Penna.

The Wimmer Lecture

DURING the centenary year of Saint Vincent Archabbey and College the Board of Trustees of the College established an annual lecture in honor of the Right Reverend Archabbot Boniface Wimmer, O.S.B. It was on October 18, 1846, that Boniface Wimmer, with his small band of pioneers, arrived at St. Vincent and began the first permanent Benedictine foundation in North America. From this Archabbey many other Benedictine abbeys have sprung, directly or indirectly. They carry on the monastic life and conduct schools and colleges in various parts of the United States and Canada.

By a memorial at once fitting and significant the Wimmer Lecture seeks to keep alive and

The Wimmer Lecture

in grateful remembrance the name of this good and great man. Each year on some convenient day near December 8, the anniversary of his death, it will bring before the members of the institution he founded a distinguished scholar, whose lecture will subsequently be printed in the form of a small book. The lecturer is free to choose his own subject.

The first Wimmer Lecture was delivered on December 7, 1947, by Professor Kenneth J. Conant, of Harvard University.

Foreword

THE series of lectures in honor of our revered founder, Boniface Wimmer, was inaugurated most happily by Professor Kenneth Conant. The subject selected by the speaker lent itself to development both illuminating and pleasantly embarrassing to listen to. Our pleasure was not diminished by the consciousness that the voice was that of an acknowledged authority.

Ripe scholarship and creative imagination enable Professor Conant to reconstruct edifices once glorious, now gone or existing only in ruins and traces. About the lofty vaults of these imaginary but authentic reconstructions he guides one with a graceful agility and surefootedness matched only by the charm with

Foreword

which he presents his discoveries. These qualities taken together render irresistible the urge to quote the felicitous pun evoked by another brilliant, seventeenth-century, bearer of the name: *Conanti nihil difficile.*

☩ Alfred Koch, O.S.B.
Archabbot and President

Illustrations

Frontispiece.
> Montecassino as rebuilt by Abbot Desiderius, 1066–77. (Restoration drawing by K. J. C.)

Figure 1.
> Rome—Old St. Peter's, 323 A.D. and later. (Restoration drawing by K. J. C.)

Figure 2.
> Tours—St. Martin, 466–70 A.D. (Diagrammatic and conjectural restoration by K. J. C.)

Figure 3.
> St. Benoît-sur-Loire—Former Abbey church, largely XI and XII centuries.

Figure 4.
> Maria Laach—Air view of the Abbey.

Figure 5.
> The St. Gall Abbey plan, redrawn and titled.

Figure 6.
> Cluny—Plan of the Abbey as of 1043. (Restoration by K. J. C.)

Illustrations

Figure 7.

St. Denis—Abbey, as of 775 A.D. (?). (Diagrammatic and conjectural restoration by K. J. C., an interpretation of material which was published by Dr. Sumner McK. Crosby, and will be restudied by him.)

Figure 8.

Centula (St. Riquier)—Abbey, as of 800 A.D. (Restoration study by K. J. C.)

Figure 9.

Tournai Cathedral, largely XII and XIII centuries.

Figure 10.

Beauvais Cathedral, with the tower of 1569. (Restoration drawing by K. J. C. on the basis of studies by Mrs. William Langton and a model by W. H. Miller, Jr.)

Figure 11.

Cluny Abbey—View from the southeast, as of 1043.

Figure 12.

Charlieu—Interior portal of the former Priory Church, c. 1080.

Illustrations

Figure 13.

   Tours—Excavations which uncovered foundations of the ambulatory and radiating chapels of the Church of St. Martin.

Figure 14.

   Tournus—Former Abbey Church of St. Philibert. Chevet, showing ambulatory and radiating chapels (979 A.D., with later additions).

Figure 15.

   Dijon—St. Bénigne, as rebuilt 1001 to c. 1025. (Restoration drawing by K. J. C. based on thesis study by Dr. Alice Sunderland and model by Howard Koeper.)

Figure 16.

   Santiago de Compostela—Cathedral. (Original scheme of 1078–1124, restored by K. J. C.)

Figure 17.

   Cluny—Third or Great Church of the monastery, 1088–XV century. (Model by Estelle Southard Hilberry; Dr. Elizabeth Sunderland, photographer.)

Figure 18.

   Cluny—Great Church. West front view. (Restoration sketch by John Savage Bolles.)

Illustrations

Figure 19.

> Cluny—Great Church. Interior of narthex (c. 1125–1225). (Drawing by Lallemand, 1787 [before the demolition].)

Figure 20.

> Cluny—Great Church. Façade of the nave as it stood before the construction of the narthex. (Model by Carter Manny; Dr. Elizabeth Sunderland, photographer; based on studies by Miss Helen Kleinschmidt and K. J. C.)

Figure 21.

> Cluny—Great Church. Section of narthex, Great Portal, and west end of the nave. (Restoration by K. J. C.)

Figure 22.

> St. Denis—Scheme of Abbot Suger's façade. (Restoration study by K. J. C.; the north tower was built differently, and has been demolished.)

Figure 23.

> Cluny—Interior of the Great Church. (Restoration by K. J. C., based on a model by T. W. D. Wright; Dr. Elizabeth Sunderland, photographer.)

Figure 24.

> Cluny—Section of the nave of the Great Church, looking east. (Restoration by K. J. C.)

Illustrations

Figure 25.
> Cluny—Plan of the sanctuary of the Great Church, 1088–95 and later; with iconographical scheme.

Figure 26.
> Cluny—Ambulatory capital from the Great Church. Charity. (Marcel Loury, photographer.)

Figure 27.
> Cluny—Ambulatory capital from the Great Church. The Fourth Tone of Plainsong. (Marcel Loury, photographer.)

Figure 28.
> Berzé-la-Ville—Chapel of former Cluniac obedience—Christ in Glory (fresco).

Figure 29.
> Cluny—Ambulatory arcade of the Great Church, with allegorical capitals. (Restored by K. J. C. over photograph of a full size reproduction in the Fogg Museum, Harvard University.)

THE BENEDICTINE WAY OF LIFE IS a great legacy from Antiquity. There is something grandly Roman, in the best and largest sense, in the figure of Saint Benedict himself—monastic patriarch, lawgiver, architect of the lives and devotions of myriads of followers throughout forty generations. He put his seal upon the monastic institution, not by some fiat, but by the practical, intellectual, and spiritual character of the Rule which he worked out for his own monastery at Montecassino. Saint Benedict's Rule, spreading everywhere in Western Christendom on its own merits, brought into being a great and stable institution which offered a safe refuge for the spiritual treasure of ancient times, and formed a strong base from which characteristic mediæval movements could take their start.

Benedictine Contributions

The Romans were great in precept, and Saint Benedict was no exception. His Rule is epitomized in the Benedictine motto *Ora et labora*. What better precept could there be in the disturbed late Roman period and the Dark Ages? Benedictine prayers gave a spiritual tincture to the epoch, and the labor of the Benedictines laid much of the economic foundation on which early mediæval progress was built. The precept *Ora et labora* guaranteed a fine architectural development from the very fact that the communities were communities at work, and it guaranteed an excellent church architecture because the most precious function of the communities was in prayer.

It is our task to examine the Benedictine contributions to church architecture, and we shall find that their achievement was glorious indeed. The needs and the hopes of the Bene-

To Church Architecture

dictines gave form to a great style of architecture, the Romanesque, which is the monastic style par excellence, flowering in the eleventh century, at the time when the Abbey of Montecassino itself was revived and rebuilt with splendid decorations by Abbot Desiderius, later Pope Victor III (frontispiece). Furthermore, we shall find that the Romanesque inheritance of Gothic architecture is of basic significance for that splendid cathedral style.

What I call "the Earliest Christian architecture" flourished in the 250 years before the Persecution of Diocletian. Such as it was, it was the work of individual communities of Christian believers, mostly in the Roman empire and subject to the conditions of contemporary Græco-Roman architecture. The growth of the new cult made no demands which the ordinary classic architecture of the

Benedictine Contributions

time was unable to supply. We know that the Earliest Christian architecture was relatively unimportant because Diocletian was able to bring about its almost complete destruction in a brief period during the great persecution of the years 303–304.

Constantine's reversal of Diocletian's anti-Christian policy entailed a rapid reconstruction, and the new status of the church as an official organ of Imperial society meant vast imperial patronage. Thereupon church architecture became a new and outstanding problem for the imperial architects, and they put the stamp of imperial grandeur upon it. The resulting style is called Early Christian. The most influential example in Western Christendom was the old basilica of St. Peter's in the Vatican, begun in 323 (figure 1). I think it is quite clear that Desiderius' architect was in-

To Church Architecture

spired by this great building, and its influence is clearly traceable in many other churches of importance. The grand axis with its extensions measured about 900 Roman feet and the transept 300; the nave was about 200 Roman feet wide, with a main central space in the nave measuring 300 Roman feet in length by 80 in width, and 120 in height. Great Early Christian churches began to appear in Eastern Christendom almost immediately. Work was begun in 326 on the first church of the Holy Sepulchre in Jerusalem, dedicated in 335, and a fine rotunda was built there over the tomb of Christ before 347. Beginning about 330 an imposing octagonal cathedral some 150 feet in diameter was built at Antioch and many churches of lesser importance were built throughout the Roman world.

By 450 the victory of Christianity was as-

Benedictine Contributions

sured, and conditions changed somewhat. It was during the fifth century that the cities quite literally emptied into the churches. Through their increasing prestige, the bishops became leaders in the great task of multiplying and enlarging the churches everywhere.

In this whole episode of Early Christian architecture under imperial and episcopal patronage, masonry vaulting, except in the apses, was rare. The emperors in the East Roman Empire, beginning with Justinian, brought about the creation of Byzantine architecture through the application of essentially oriental vaulting methods to essentially Roman church plans. The first monument of Byzantine architecture was Saint Sophia in Constantinople, built at the command of Justinian, beginning in 532 and dedicated in 537 and 563. The true line of Byzantine architecture

To Church Architecture

was marked out by this building, and in Eastern Christendom court patronage has continued to motivate the construction of churches having essentially this same character almost to the present day.

The period from 450 to the middle of the sixth century was similarly decisive for church architecture in the West. The church of St. Martin built between 466 and 470 over the grave of the soldierly first bishop of Tours by a successor, Perpetuus, has long since been destroyed, but archæological studies clearly indicate that it was one of the first occidental churches to show characteristic mediæval tendencies (figure 2). The nave and sanctuary were basilican in form, and were horizontal in movement, as classic designs usually are, but that classic horizontalism was contradicted by a lantern tower and belfry called a *turritus*

Benedictine Contributions

apex. The *turritus apex* provided a strong vertical accent, and in fact it is the progenitor of the mediæval church spire. St. Martin's also had a vestibule tower which is described as if it were capable of defense (*"haec tuta turris"*). This is clearly one of the early examples of a strong functional elaboration at the main front of a church, and of course the belfry pinnacle (*"unde [Martinus] vocat populos"*) as well as the lantern tower (which gave a flood of light before the altar) were functional elements also.

In 543 before St. Sophia in Constantinople was finally completed, St. Maur brought Benedictinism to France; he died in 565, the year of Justinian's death, two years after St. Sophia was finished. Glanfeuil, St. Maur's monastery, was in the Loire region, near Saumur, and within two or three generations after St.

To Church Architecture

Maur's death, St. Martin at Tours in that same valley had become a Benedictine monastery. St. Martin's was taken over by canons in 816–17, but for nearly two centuries it was one of the most important Benedictine centres. The fact that St. Martin's church was an interesting building is important for architecture and for the Benedictines. The basic design of the church was one which was capable of inventive development as need arose, and knowledge of it was widely spread by multifarious Benedictine contacts, which included the famous pilgrimage to St. Martin's tomb. In this way, unquestionably, the design imprinted itself on the artistic consciousness of the time, and did its part in the creation of the accepted formula of the mediæval monastic church building. How this imprint was carried through the centuries is revealed in the bold

Benedictine Contributions

and handsome silhouette of the church of St. Benoît-sur-Loire (figure 3). This noble Romanesque building, which according to one tradition contains the actual remains of St. Benedict brought long ago from Montecassino, is a wonderful work of the eleventh and twelfth centuries, beautifully constructed on a grand scale with masonry vaulting and otherwise elaborated. Its architectural theme is the same as that of St. Martin's. The elaborations and improvements are an indication of what the Benedictines did for ecclesiastical architecture in the intervening six hundred years.

It is not always realized that during the early Middle Ages of Western Christendom monastic architecture was the only living and growing architecture. The Benedictine monks were by temperament admirably suited to conserve what could be saved of the tradition

To Church Architecture

of ancient architecture, but their very success engendered two architectural problems which were unsolved in antiquity. First there was the new problem of the great, nearly self-sufficient monastic community establishment, serving as shrine, residence, storehouse and manufactory for as many sometimes as a thousand members, serving also as spiritual, intellectual, and agricultural capital for its region. Second, there was the new problem of the highly articulated monastic church, often a place of pilgrimage, and wherever possible a substantial fireproof building. In what follows we shall see that the Benedictines achieved admirable solutions in both fields.

The problem of the monastic group was early solved by elaborating the scheme of the ancient Roman villa. The Benedictine reform movement of the time of Charlemagne pro-

Benedictine Contributions

duced, in 822, the type plan which is preserved in the library of St. Gall (figure 5). A purely cursory glance shows it to be an orderly arrangement, on a grand scale, of the functional units of a complex and flourishing organization. The scheme may be followed, with slight variations, through the famous eleventh-century plan of Cluny (figure 6), on into Cistercian, Gothic and Renaissance architecture, and indeed to modern times. When, as at Cluny, the buildings have been lost, but not their plan, it is a comparatively simple matter to restore their general form (figure 11), because the preserved remains are so simple, so straightforward, and so characterful. The mediæval spirit still lives and moves and is perceptible in buildings and decorations of Renaissance and even modern date, at Maria Laach in Germany (figure 4), where the old

To Church Architecture

Benedictinism has returned to flourish as it did in the Middle Ages.

These monastic groups, like any well-built buildings in which work is done, are intrinsically interesting. A logical system of reduplicating quadrangles was employed with great skill in accommodating the residential and service units. Accidents of history, terrain, and imagination produced a fascinating variety in these courts and cloisters, and their embellishments of painting and sculpture were often of a high order of merit.

It is to be noted, and we see it at Maria Laach (and equally at St. Vincent Archabbey), that this mundane side of the Benedictine existence produced vast spreading architectural compositions of horizontal character. But in spite of their considerable size, they are dominated by the church buildings. In the precept

Benedictine Contributions

Ora et labora a sure instinct has put the emphasis on prayer. The great bulk and imposing form of the Benedictine church buildings is an apt expression of this in architectural terms. With unerring sentiment the Benedictines multiplied and elaborated the vertical elements in the church fabric, and thus created some of the most impressive compositions in all religious architecture. This achievement was also taken over by Gothic builders, and it underlies some of their most striking successes.

The developments began immediately under the Carolingians in the first period of relative prosperity after the Dark Ages. Pepin the Short and Charlemagne built the royal Benedictine abbey church of Saint Denis near Paris, and this building, dedicated (according to the legend by Christ himself) in 775, al-

To Church Architecture

ready has something of the dynamic character which characterized our Western church architecture until the Neo-classic period. Many details of the Saint Denis design of 775 are irrecoverable, but it is not open to doubt that the whole composition piled up to a central lantern motive, while the west front had a bold axial projection, later reduced to a pair of towers, as seen in figure 7. The building survived with little further change until about 1140, when the two ends were rebuilt in enlarged form by the famous Abbot Suger.

Another Benedictine monastery church which greatly interested Charlemagne was that of Centula or St. Riquier in northern France, where a close family relative, Angilbert, was abbot. Charlemagne contributed large funds toward the construction and personally attended one of the dedications, which

Benedictine Contributions

took place in 799 and 800 (figure 8). The building has been destroyed, but it is known through reproductions of an eleventh century miniature. Its whole design acquired a tremendous dynamism through the use of reduplicated and augmented tower forms. The atrium, for example, had three entrances, each with a tower, and each of these towers was augmented by a chapel in the upper story. The vestibule of the church had a large chapel above it, and this chapel was elaborated as a veritable tower church with galleries and a remarkable wooden telescopic openwork spire, which was itself an augmentation of the ancient *turritus apex*. The chapel was further dignified by flanking cylindrical stair turrets, and these latter blossomed in openwork spirelets. This design presents the oldest really imposing church façade of which we have

To Church Architecture

knowledge, and it is therefore of the utmost importance to the history of form in church architecture. We pay it an instinctive compliment every time we see a church with a bold and handsome spire over the main door, as in Trinity Church at the head of Wall Street, New York. The telescopic *turritus apex* and stair towers were repeated at the crossing of St. Riquier, so that the complete composition possessed nine towers, and an energetic silhouette of new and special character.

The nine-towered church became a notable theme in Romanesque and Gothic architecture. The design for the cathedral of Tournai (figure 9), never fully completed, was perhaps the most striking example. The cathedrals of Laon, Chartres, and Reims were intended to have similar tower groups, but these ensembles were never carried very far toward com-

Benedictine Contributions

pletion. The crossing tower scheme undoubtedly came to culmination in the phenomenal 501-foot staged tower and spire of the Cathedral of Beauvais (completed in 1569 and little known because it fell in 1573; figure 10). This was an amazing later version, in stone except for the flèche, of the *turritus apex* at St. Riquier.

A new period of prosperity opened for the Benedictines in 910 with the foundation of the reforming abbey of Cluny in Burgundy. The spiritual life of this great institute was brought to its full power by the renowned Odo, former precentor of St. Martin of Tours, who became abbot in 927. Its first church was dedicated by 927; the growth of the abbey soon called for a second church, which was built between 955 and 981, and apparently vaulted by the year 1000, when the Benedictines were having

To Church Architecture

their first success with vaulted architecture (figure 11). Being of solider construction than St. Riquier, Cluny was soberer in general design, but the plan as we know it from a description of 1043 (figure 6), was actually more interesting, for functional reasons. The Cluniac Lord's Day liturgy called for a procession from the high altar around the cloister of the monastery, with various stations, including one before the main door of the church. Near the close of this the head of the procession went on before into the church, as Christ before his disciples into Galilee. From this "Galilee" station of the Cluniac liturgy (then very influential) arose an interesting development of "Galilee" vestibules or ante-churches, and also (at Charlieu, about 1080, figure 12) the custom of placing Resurrection iconography on the main doorway of the church

Benedictine Contributions

nave. Out of this scheme the gorgeous idea of the sculptural church portal was gradually developed. Magnificent ensembles like those of the Gothic cathedrals of Chartres, Amiens, and Paris actually depend on a Romanesque and Benedictine inheritance.

The second church of Cluny also shows architectural progress in the elaborate plan of its east end. With increasing numbers of priests among the monks, the need rose for extra chapels. There are traces of several ninth-century examples showing various interesting combinations of chapels arranged ladderwise—in echelon—about the principal apse, with access corridors. It is commonly believed that the first regular semicircular corridor with radiating chapels was built at Saint Martin of Tours (then a collegiate church) in the tenth century (figure 13). This improved

To Church Architecture

version of an old Benedictine arrangement was soon taken up in the Order. The oldest example now existing, dated 979, is in the crypt of the former Benedictine abbey church of Tournus near Cluny (figure 14). The third abbey church at Cluny itself, of which we shall speak later, had a splendid Romanesque apse with ambulatory and radiating chapels dating from 1088 (figure 17). The finest Romanesque examples are Benedictine.

The gorgeous series of Gothic churches with this beautiful feature culminates in the Cathedral of Beauvais (1227–1325, figure 10), but it begins with Abbot Suger's works, already mentioned, at the old Benedictine royal abbey church of St. Denis. And here it was that the old idea of colored glass windows was developed by Abbot Suger with a characteristic Benedictine combination of thought and

Benedictine Contributions

feeling, into the iconographical, almost liturgical system of stained glass windows with devotional subjects. And, one may add, basic progress in the creation of the Gothic structural system was made in this same church at the same time, about 1140.

Let us turn backward and see something of the stages which underlie this great development. By the year 1000 the Benedictines were ready to realize highly evolved designs, with these elaborate elements, in fireproof structure. Their Roman way of thinking and their stability made these monks wish instinctively for solid vaulted construction. Engineering skill was able, at the beginning of the eleventh century, to fulfill their desire.

In the first twenty-five years of the eleventh century, the church of Saint Bénigne was built for the abbey of that name in Dijon, under

To Church Architecture

Saint William (figure 15). It was entirely covered by vaults of the Roman type, and it was in effect a museum of the various features of church architecture which had been developing during the preceding five hundred years—basilica, rotunda, crypt, galleries, apse, ambulatory, echelons of chapels, towers—all in an array which was wonderful for the time, though inexperience was perceptible in the ponderous fabric of certain parts and in the rather uncontrolled exuberance of the architectural composition.

How half a century of esthetic effort gave cogency to such compositions and synthesis to the Romanesque style as a whole may be seen in the design of the Cathedral of Santiago de Compostela (figure 16), as begun in 1078. This, the most magnificent Romanesque church in Spain, was built in collaboration

Benedictine Contributions

with, and was partly owned by, a Benedictine monastery; moreover it represents the style as worked out at this period among the Benedictines of France. We are reminded by this circumstance, in which a great cathedral borrows from monastic architecture, that the latter was still the living and growing architecture in Western Christendom, with other types of building drawing upon the monastic style. This is also true of the fine cathedral buildings which were being built at the time in England and Germany.

Noble as Santiago Cathedral is, it was not the masterpiece of Romanesque architecture; that distinction was reserved for the third Abbey church of Cluny (figure 17 ff.), the largest of monastic and of Romanesque churches, and the most representative in every way of the style. It was, so to speak, the

To Church Architecture

capital church of the widely ramified Cluniac Congregation of Benedictines; it was built under Saint Hugh of Semur when that strong group of Benedictine houses was at the height of its power and effectiveness. In this church of 1088 to 1225 (with less important later additions), it was once possible to gauge, better than anywhere else, the greatness of the Benedictine contribution to mediæval church architecture. By a calamitous misfortune the building was demolished between 1798 and 1811, but extensive archæological studies sponsored by the Mediæval Academy of America have given back the lineaments of the church, so that in imagination we may visit it.

The outer entrance to the abbey was through a double portal resembling a city gate, and reminiscent of the Roman heritage of

Benedictine Contributions

Benedictine monasticism. The huge western towers were finished in Romanesque during the fifteenth century, a testimony to the durable affection in which the monks held their own traditional style (figure 18). The extended axis of the building, measuring 615 English or 635 Roman feet, made the composition a horizontal one, but its silhouette was broken dramatically by the vertical accents of seven towers.

Upon entering the visitor discovered a Galilee or ante-church which was begun about 1125 and finished about 1225. The interior had Romanesque proportions, but Gothic construction (figures 19, 21). It is probable that the oldest parts of the ante-church influenced the Abbot Suger of Saint Denis when he added a narthex and towers to the old Carolingian building which we have men-

To Church Architecture

tioned, intending to transform it into the first of all Gothic churches.

At the head of the ante-church at Cluny there were three carved portals exemplifying another great Benedictine gift to religious architecture (figures 20, 21). They were chiseled about 1110 and soon polychromed. The central doorway was adorned with Resurrection and Apocalyptic iconography which was related liturgically, as we have seen, to the Galilee processional station. The Benedictines had now developed sculptors who could present the heavenly vision with singular power and conviction. Later portals, with other iconographical subjects, are often very impressive, but they rarely attain the majesty and force of the finest Romanesque designs.

The main portal at Cluny, one of the oldest, always remained one of the most impressive of

Benedictine Contributions

all. It had Christ blessing, vested in a great red mantle and set against a mandorla with a gilded background surrounded by angels, apocalyptic beasts, Elders and Apostles, among whom the St. Peter has been preserved, and is now in a museum at Providence, Rhode Island. The company on the Mount of Olives and other Resurrection scenes were presented on the lintel, with more abstract designs elsewhere. The whole central portal was sixty-two feet in height.

By chance the front of the main church stood free for an interval of about fifteen years beside the older church, which presented an early Romanesque example of the exterior façade with two towers. It was perhaps through this circumstance that architects came to realize for the first time what a magnificent embellishment portals would be on the exterior

To Church Architecture

façade of a great church. Almost immediately the Benedictines began, as at Vézelay and La Charité-sur-Loire, to build imposing Romanesque façades with paired towers and carved portals. This wonderful new motive enters the Gothic stylistic vocabulary at Saint Denis (figure 22), to be developed and exploited later in a marvelous series of cathedral designs, of which Notre Dame in Paris is perhaps the best known and most beloved.

At mox surgit basilica ingens—"And suddenly a giant basilica surges up," says the chronicler as he passes with the visitor from the narthex at Cluny to the nave. And indeed it was so. With a width of $33\frac{1}{3}$ Roman feet (exceptional for the time) the central nave rose a height of 100 Roman feet—the first vaulted church in Western Christendom to reach that goal. The interior was entirely Romanesque in style,

Benedictine Contributions

but it achieved the tall proportions and the inspiring verticality which we find in the noblest Gothic designs (figure 23).

The lithe aspiring effect was enhanced by numerous pointed arches, here used in profusion for the first time in any church building, and in this we have a further gift from Benedictine Romanesque to the later style, where it became important for practical as well as esthetic reasons. The symbolic significance of this aspiring quality was appreciated at the time. A Cluniac monk who knew the church when it was newly built said that to worship there was like celebrating Easter every day. I am sure that we understand what he intended to convey.

The huge nave was laid out with the considerable length of 450 Roman feet in order to provide an impressive setting for the Cluniac

To Church Architecture

liturgical processions, one of which, occurring in conjunction with the Chapter General of 1132, had 1212 monks in line. The acoustics of the church are reported as magnificent, and fortunately so, for the Cluniacs excelled in liturgical song. Actually, monastic Romanesque architecture is superior to Gothic for the chant, and the effects here, with hundreds of monks in choir, must have been overwhelming.

The great interior height at Cluny prevented the monks' choir enclosure at the head of the nave from blocking up the noble axial vista toward the high altar. A visitor to the church as he moved eastward thither would be conscious of the vast western transept, with its fine chapels, and the boldly staged eastern transept, also provided with a series of chapels; but his gaze would inevitably be

Benedictine Contributions

drawn to the main apse, with its ambulatory and its corona of radiating chapels, the boldest and most impressive in all Romanesque building (figures 17, 24, 25). Only scattered parts of it now exist, but long and careful study has done much toward recreating its glory. The matutinal altar slab of marble and parts of the nine-foot high jasper high altar slab have been recognized, and it is known that they were consecrated by the Cluniac Pope Urban II, former grand Prior of Cluny, on October 25th, 1095. At that time only the eastern parts of the church were complete.

On the lofty vault of the apse there was a vast fresco painting of Christ in Glory, resembling the contemporary one which still survives at nearby Berzé-la-Ville (figures 23, 28). Both were noble French examples affected by the splendid Benedictine revival of

page thirty-two

To Church Architecture

mural painting which took place at Montecassino under Abbot Desiderius. The celestial vision was placed, with perfect symbolism, directly above the altar, and it dominated the whole interior of the nave by its majesty.

On the capitals of the slender shafts which made such a graceful semicircle about the altars, there were allegorical carvings. The designs were of touching beauty. Their loveliness exemplified the new style of sculptural decoration created in the eleventh century, as another gift which the Benedictines gave to church architecture, after developing it from crude beginnings. The work in the apse at Cluny went beyond mere carving, for the subjects were arranged according to a definite iconographical scheme (figure 25). Such ordered schemes are of capital importance in mediæval art, and this work at Cluny is an

Benedictine Contributions

early example. Abbot Suger elaborated his famous stained glass windows already mentioned according to such ideas, and in the end they made the Gothic cathedral the "Bible of the Poor." The world owes the Benedictines a great debt of gratitude for initiating this development.

It was, then, one of the first important mediæval allegories in sculpture which was carved on the beautiful capitals (still existing) which were ranged about the altars at Cluny. The allegory has an affecting simplicity and directness. At the extreme left there was a capital representing our First Parents and their disobedience in Paradise; at the other extremity the Sacrifice of Abraham, prefiguring the Christian Sacrifice which took place every day on the two altars between. Intervening capitals had beautiful figures to repre-

To Church Architecture

sent the monastic life with its struggles and joys, its virtues, it labors, and its praises. Of particular charm are the figures representing the Virtues (figure 26) and the Tones of Plainsong (figures 27, 29), the sweet savor and the rich spiritual harvest of monastic devotion. Such a lovely allegory was quite in its place at the culminating point of a Benedictine church, for the Benedictines have always offered Our Lord a fine intellectuality along with their incense and their prayers.

It is clear from what has been said that art-lovers in general far underestimate the contribution which the Benedictines made to mediæval church building. When in the sixth century they took over from the bishops the leading role in Western architecture, the typical works were Classic architecture with

Benedictine Contributions

only an incipient mediævalism. The Benedictines essayed and developed a great many of the most important, most conspicuous, and most beloved features of church architecture. When it was the bishops' turn to take over again in the middle of the twelfth century, the monks gave them the new Gothic architecture, with a rich background of Romanesque motives which had an extraordinary future in the Gothic style.

It might be said that the bishops were not themselves responsible for the Gothic buildings because underlings designed and built them. But the bishops knew their architecture, knew their problem, and knew their age. Their leadership was essential, and it joined all the forces of the community, including the craftsmen, to produce the great result.

To Church Architecture

The same is true, and in relatively larger measure, of the Benedictine centuries. The actual needs of the Benedictine communities called forth the buildings and their elaborations. Many who played essential roles in the history of Benedictine architecture and decoration are known to have been monks or brothers, but it is a fact that essential work was done by lay people in Benedictine employ.

Yet the quality of all the old Benedictine architecture is monastic. It invariably has the virtues which monks admire, and the atmosphere in which they are at home. To my mind this is an excellent tribute to the Benedictines themselves, and their ample spirit, which every church historian instinctively recognizes. In that large and rich ambient the designer and craftsman, cleric or lay, happily and willingly submerged his individuality to

Benedictine Contributions

participate in the *Opus Dei* of the monks by his work with the chisel, trowel, or brush. This occurred everywhere, and it put a special mark on the buildings. Today, even where the shrines are in other hands or ruined and desolate, with their sculptures broken, the warm envelope of kindly Benedictine devotion lingers—imparting the age-old message which is living and fresh wherever the Benedictines tread.

Selected Bibliography

ALBERT EDWARD BAILEY, editor: *The Arts and Religion.* Macmillan, 1944
Contains an essay by the present author.

FRANCIS BOND: *Gothic Architecture in England.* Batsford, 1906
Inclusive and authoritative work, giving the background of Gothic in England, as well as the Gothic monuments themselves, with many illustrations.

ALFRED W. CLAPHAM: *Romanesque Architecture in Western Europe.* Oxford, Clarendon Press, 1936
Authoritative presentation by one of the best English architectural historians; in small compass but readable and well illustrated.

KENNETH JOHN CONANT: *A Brief Commentary on Early Mediaeval Church Architecture, with Especial Reference to Lost Monuments.* The Johns Hopkins Press, 1942
Self-explanatory title; many illustrations.

Bibliography

CAMILLE ENLART: *Manuel d'Archéologie française*. Paris, Picard, 1919 ff. (revised edition)

A series of careful analytical volumes, with lists, and excellent illustrations of structural features. The sections on monastic and civil architecture are interesting.

JOAN EVANS: *Monastic Life at Cluny 910–1157*. Oxford University Press, 1931

A beautiful short presentation by an eminent English mediævalist and lover of Cluniac art.

JOAN EVANS: *Romanesque Architecture of the Order of Cluny*. Cambridge University Press, 1938

A monumental work, with remarkable lists of the Cluniac possessions, an excellent analysis of the architecture, and nearly 300 illustrations.

JOAN EVANS: *Art in Mediaeval France*. Oxford University Press, 1948

A remarkable and beautiful achievement, which gives due attention to monastic art in a singularly clear and well-ordered presentation; 281 illustrations of fine quality.

page forty

Bibliography

PAUL FRANKL: *Baukunst des Mittelalters; die frühmittelalterliche und romanische Baukunst.* Wildpark-Potsdam, Academische Verlagsgesellschaft Athenaion, 1926
Well-studied and well-illustrated book of rather technical cast.

ARTHUR GARDNER: *An Introduction to French Church Architecture.* Macmillan, 1938
A short general text, plus tabloid monographs, one with each of the many and systematically chosen illustrations. A good book.

ROBERT DE LASTEYRIE: *L'Architecture religieuse en France à l'époque romane.* Paris, Picard, 1929 (revised edition)
A fine work of French erudition, amply illustrated.

VIOLET R. MARKHAM: *Romanesque France.* Dutton, 1929
Abounds in interesting descriptive and biographical material, but the archæological material is somewhat subject to caution.

REXFORD NEWCOMB: *Outlines of the History of Architecture,* especially parts II (1932) and IV. Wiley, 1934
Analyses, lists, topographical material, information on materials and engineering problems.

Bibliography

ARTHUR KINGSLEY PORTER: *Medieval Architecture—Its Origin and Development.* Baker and Taylor, 1909

An early work of the eminent mediævalist, and in some ways to be used with caution, but notable for a polyglot bibliography and a long series of short descriptive notes on the monuments.

ERNEST H. SHORT: *The House of God.* Macmillan, 1926

A substantial volume treating the great architecture of the several important religions from antiquity to the present; somewhat encyclopædic in its manner, it nevertheless reads easily, and is fairly dependable.

Illustrations

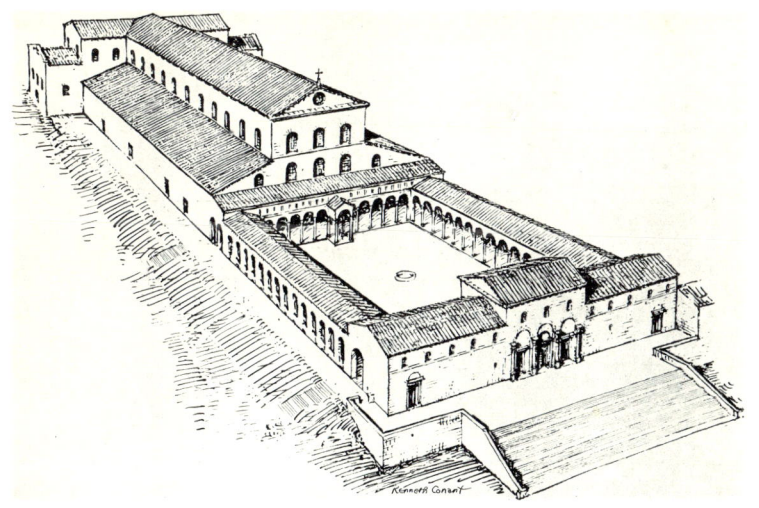

Figure 1. Rome—Old St. Peter's, 323 A.D. and later. (Restoration drawing by K. J. C.)

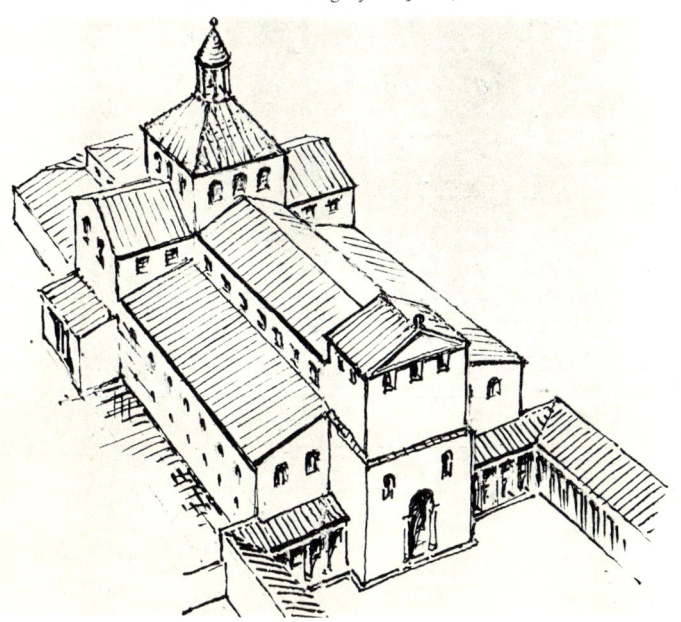

Figure 2. Tours — St. Martin, 466–70 A.D. (Diagrammatic and conjectural restoration by K. J. C.)

page forty-five

Figure 3. St. Benoît-sur-Loire — Former Abbey church, largely XI and XII centuries.

Figure 4. Maria Laach — Air view of the Abbey.

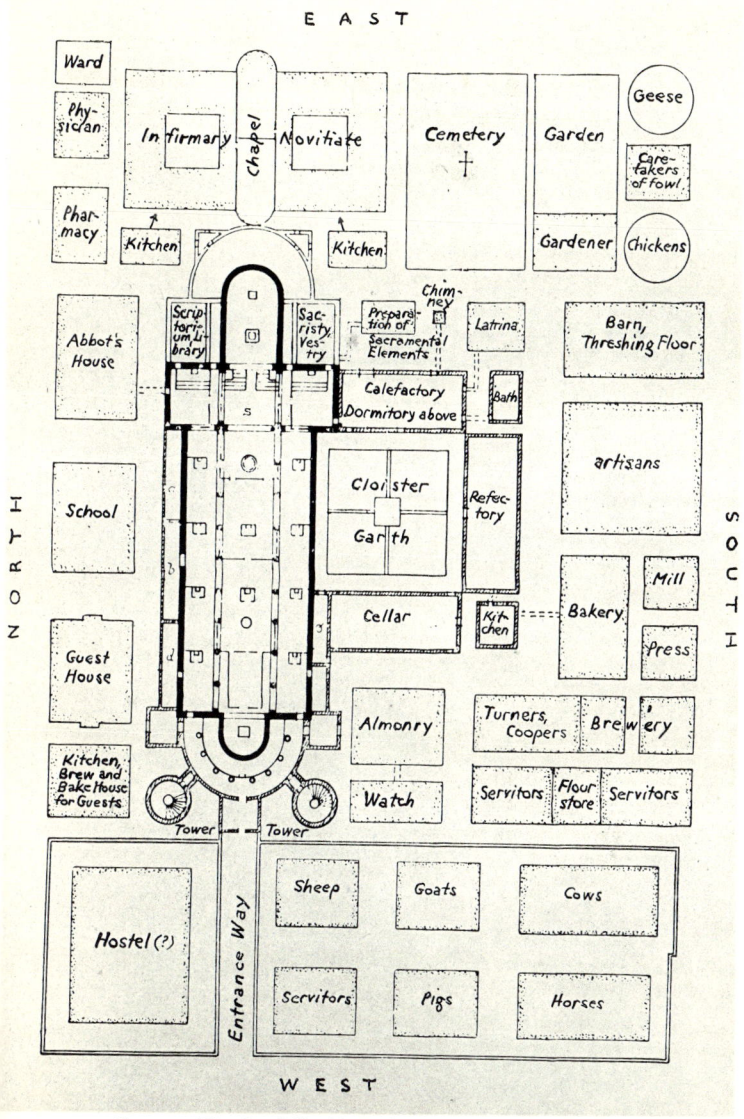

Figure 5. The St. Gall Abbey plan, redrawn and titled.

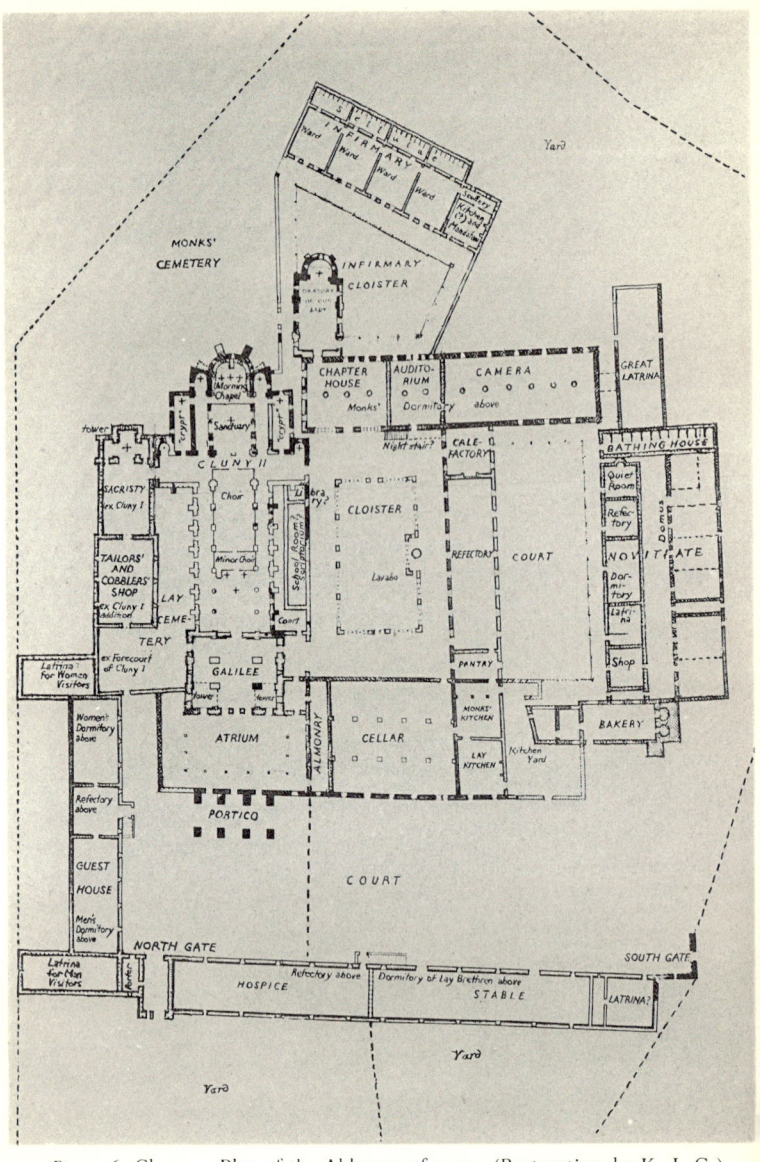

Figure 6. Cluny — Plan of the Abbey as of 1043. (Restoration by K. J. C.)

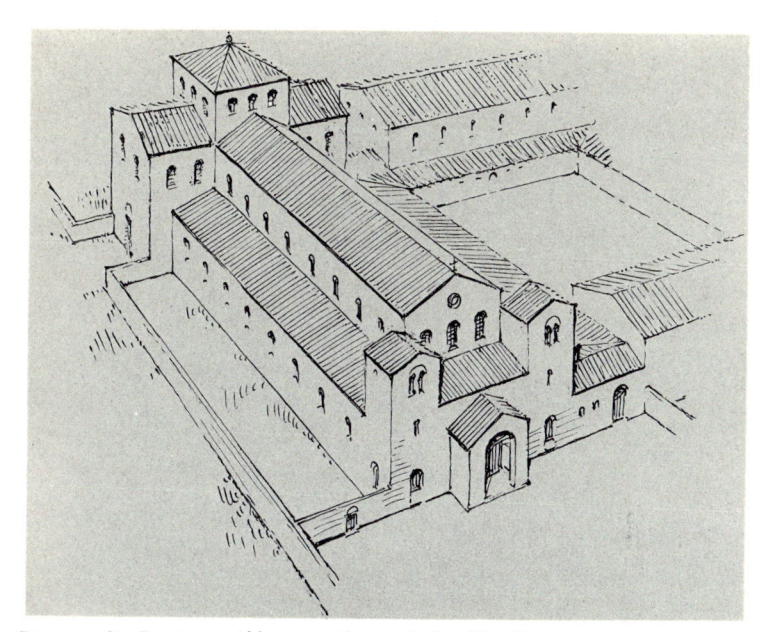

Figure 7. St. Denis — Abbey, as of 775 A.D. (?). (Diagrammatic and conjectural restoration by K. J. C., an interpretation of material which was published by Dr. Sumner McK. Crosby, and will be restudied by him.)

Figure 8. Centula (St. Riquier) — Abbey, as of 800 A.D. (Restoration study by K. J. C.)

page forty-nine

Figure 9. Tournai Cathedral, largely XII and XIII centuries.

Figure 10. Beauvais Cathedral, with the tower of 1569. (Restoration drawing by K. J. C. on the basis of studies by Mrs. William Langton and a model by W. H. Miller, Jr.)

Figure 11. Cluny Abbey — View from the southeast, as of 1043.

Figure 12. Charlieu — Interior portal of the former Priory Church, c. 1080.

Figure 13. Tours—Excavations which uncovered foundations of the ambulatory and radiating chapels of the church of St. Martin.

Figure 14. Tournus — Former Abbey Church of St. Philibert. Chevet, showing ambulatory and radiating chapels (979 A.D., with later additions).

page fifty-three

Figure 15. Dijon — St. Bénigne, as rebuilt 1001 to c. 1025. (Restoration drawing by K. J. C. based on thesis study by Dr. Alice Sunderland and model by Howard Koeper.)

Figure 16. Santiago de Compostela — Cathedral. (Original scheme of 1078–1124, restored by K. J. C.)

Figure 17. Cluny — Third or Great Church of the monastery, 1088–XV century. (Model by Estelle Southard Hilberry; Dr. Elizabeth Sunderland, photographer.)

page fifty-five

Figure 18. Cluny — Great Church. West front view. (Restoration sketch by John Savage Bolles.)

Figure 19. Cluny — Great Church. Interior of narthex (c. 1125–1225). (Drawing by Lallemand, 1787 [before the demolition].)

Figure 20. Cluny — Great Church. Façade of the nave as it stood before the construction of the narthex. (Model by Carter Manny; Dr. Elizabeth Sunderland, photographer; based on studies by Miss Helen Kleinschmidt and K. J. C.)

Figure 21. Cluny — Great Church. Section of narthex, Great Portal, and west end of the nave. (Restoration by K. J. C.)

page fifty-eight

Figure 22. St. Denis — Scheme of Abbot Suger's façade. (Restoration study by K. J. C.; the north tower was built differently, and has been demolished.)

Figure 23. Cluny — Interior of the Great Church. (Restoration by K. J. C., based on a model by T. W. D. Wright; Dr. Elizabeth Sunderland, photographer.)

Figure 24. Cluny — Section of the nave of the Great Church, looking East. (Restoration by K. J. C.)

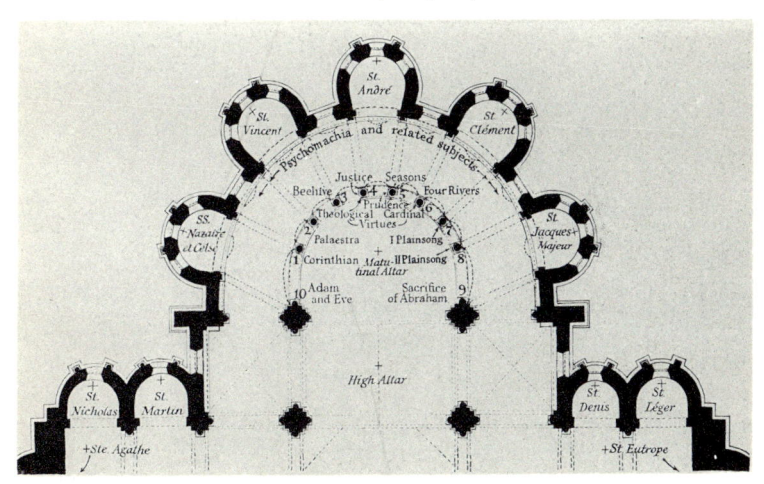

Figure 25. Cluny — Plan of the sanctuary of the Great Church, 1088-95 and later; with iconographical scheme.

page sixty-one

Figure 26. Cluny — Ambulatory capital from the Great Church. Charity. (Marcel Loury, photographer.)

Figure 27. Cluny — Ambulatory capital from the Great Church. The Fourth Tone of Plainsong. (Marcel Loury, photographer.)

Figure 28. Berzé-la-Ville — Chapel of former Cluniac obedience — Christ in Glory (fresco).

Figure 29. Cluny — Ambulatory arcade of the Great Church, with allegorical capitals. (Restored by K. J. C. over photograph of a full size reproduction in the Fogg Museum, Harvard University.)

page sixty-three